**JOHN STOTT BIBLE**

*10 Studies with Commentary for Individuals or Groups*

# 1 & 2
# Thessalonians

## Living in the End Times

John
## STOTT

### with Dale and Sandy Larsen

Inter-Varsity Press
Nottingham, England

**IVP** Connect
An imprint of InterVarsity Press
Downers Grove, Illinois

InterVarsity Press, USA
P.O. Box 1400, Downers Grove, IL 60515-1426, USA
World Wide Web: www.ivpress.com
Email: email@ivpress.com

Inter-Varsity Press, England
Norton Street, Nottingham NG7 3HR, England
Website: www.ivpbooks.com
Email: ivp@ivpbooks.com

InterVarsity Press®, USA, is the book-publishing division of InterVarsity Christian Fellowship/USA®,
a movement of students and faculty active on campus at hundreds of universities, colleges and schools
of nursing in the United States of America, and a member movement of the International Fellowship of
Evangelical Students. For information about local and regional activities, write Public Relations Dept.,
InterVarsity Christian Fellowship/USA, 6400 Schroeder Rd., P.O. Box 7895, Madison, WI 53707-7895,
or visit the IVCF website at <www.intervarsity.org>.

Inter-Varsity Press, England, is closely linked with the Universities and Colleges Christian Fellowship, a
student movement connecting Christian Unions in universities and colleges throughout Great Britain, and
a member movement of the International Fellowship of Evangelical Students. Website: www.uccf.org.uk.

This study guide is based on and includes excerpts adapted from The Message of 1 & 2 Thessalonians
©1991 by John R. W. Stott, originally published in the U.S. under the title The Gospel and the End of
Time.

Design: Cindy Kiple
Images: © Kuzma/iStockphoto

USA ISBN 978-0-8308-2166-2
UK ISBN 978-1-84474-320-9

Printed in the United States of America ∞

P   23   22   21   20   19   18   17   16   15   14   13   12   11   10   9   8   7   6   5   4

Y   30   29   28   27   26   25   24   23   22   21   20   19   18   17   16   15   14   13   12

Introducing 1 & 2 Thessalonians ———————— 5

1/   1 Thessalonians 1
     PASSING IT ON ————————————— 9

2/   1 Thessalonians 2:1-16
     PLEASING GOD———————————— 14

3/   1 Thessalonians 2:17—3:13
     DOUBLE COMMITMENT ——————— 19

4/   1 Thessalonians 4:1-12
     LIVING THE GOSPEL————————— 24

5/   1 Thessalonians 4:13-18
     HOPE IN THE FACE OF DEATH ———— 30

6/   1 Thessalonians 5:1-11
     WAITING FOR CHRIST————————— 34

7/   1 Thessalonians 5:12-28
     CHRISTIAN COMMUNITY———————— 39

8/   2 Thessalonians 1
     DYNAMIC FAITH ————————— 44

9/   2 Thessalonians 2
     STANDING FIRM ———————— 49

10/  2 Thessalonians 3
     THE WORD OF PEACE ————————— 54

Guidelines for Leaders——————————— 59

# Introducing 1 & 2 Thessalonians

"There is a kind of unmingled sweetness in this epistle," wrote Johann Albrecht Bengel about 1 Thessalonians in the eighteenth century *(Gnomon of the New Testament)*. Indeed I have found much sweetness in both letters as, for many years now, I have reflected on their meaning and message.

These letters reveal the authentic Paul. Not that he is ever inauthentic. But sometimes the human Paul is obscured by his apostolic office and authority. To be sure, in the Thessalonian letters he issues commands and demands obedience. More often, however, he writes like the pastor he is, indeed like the Thessalonians' mother and father, which is what he claims to be (1 Thessalonians 2:7, 11). He loves them, gives himself for them, is anxiously concerned for their welfare, teaches and admonishes them, begs them to stand firm, and prays for them constantly, urgently and personally.

### About the Thessalonians
When Paul and his companions visited Thessalonica in A.D. 49 or 50, it was already a well-established city with a long history. It occupied a strategic position, for it boasted a good natural harbor at the head of the Thermaic Gulf.

Acts 17 tells the story of how Thessalonica was evangelized on Paul's second missionary journey. Due to opposition Paul and Silas had to be smuggled out of town. It was in Corinth that Paul wrote his first letter to the Thessalonian church.

The apostle responded in this letter to the information he had received from Timothy. Timothy brought good news of the Thessalonians' "faith and love" (1 Thessalonians 3:6-8). On the other hand, he had reported that Paul was being criticized (2:2-6; 2:17—3:5). In addition the Thessalonians needed correction and instruction in the areas of sexual morality, earning their own living, preparing for the second coming of Jesus and tensions in the fellowship.

It seems certain that Paul, Silas and Timothy were still in Corinth when the Thessalonians' response to Paul's first letter arrived. The news they received was mixed, as is clear from the second letter it prompted.

## A Message for Us

Like all of Paul's other letters, 1 and 2 Thessalonians are ad hoc documents, called forth by special, local circumstances to which he was responding. At the same time they contain some of the most important New Testament passages about eschatology, the culmination of all things. They set forth the Christian view of history, showing that history is linear rather than circular or cyclical, and that history will come to a planned end, a grand finale, consisting of the parousia or second coming of Christ, the resurrection, the judgment and the kingdom. We, too, are part of God's great plan in history.

## Suggestions for Individual Study

**1.** As you begin each study, pray that God will speak to you through his Word.

**2.** Read the introduction to the study and respond to the question that follows it. This is designed to help you get into the theme of the study.

**3.** The studies are written in an inductive format designed to help you discover for yourself what Scripture is saying. Each study deals with a particular passage so that you can really delve into the author's meaning in that context. Read and reread the passage to be studied. The questions are written using the language of the New International Version, so you may wish to use that version of the Bible. The New Revised Standard Version is also recommended.

**4.** Each study includes three types of questions. *Observation* questions ask about the basic facts: who, what, when, where and how.

*Interpretation* questions delve into the meaning of the passage. *Application* questions (also found in the "Apply" section) help you discover the implications of the text for growing in Christ. These three keys unlock the treasures of Scripture.

Write your answers to the study questions in the spaces provided or in a personal journal. Writing can bring clarity and deeper understanding of yourself and of God's Word.

**5.** In the studies you will find some commentary notes designed to give help with complex verses by giving further biblical and cultural background and contextual information. The notes in the studies are not designed to answer the questions for you. They are to help you along as you learn to study the Bible for yourself. After you have worked through the questions and notes in the guide, you may want to read the accompanying commentary by John Stott in the Bible Speaks Today series. This will give you more information about the text.

**6.** Move to the "Apply" section. These questions will help you connect the key biblical themes to your own life. Putting the application into practice is one of the keys to growing in Christ.

**7.** Use the guidelines in the "Pray" section to focus on God, thanking him for what you have learned and praying about the applications that have come to mind.

### Suggestions for Members of a Group Study

**1.** Come to the study prepared. Follow the suggestions for individual study mentioned above. You will find that careful preparation will greatly enrich your time spent in group discussion.

**2.** Be willing to participate in the discussion. The leader of your group will not be lecturing. Instead, she or he will be encouraging the members of the group to discuss what they have learned. The leader will be asking the questions that are found in this guide.

**3.** Stick to the topic being discussed. Your answers should be based on the verses which are the focus of the discussion and not on outside authorities such as commentaries or speakers. These studies focus on a particular passage of Scripture. Only rarely should you refer to other portions of the Bible. This allows for everyone to participate on equal ground and for in-depth study.

**4.** Be sensitive to the other members of the group. Listen attentively when they describe what they have learned. You may be surprised by their insights! Each question assumes a variety of answers. Many questions do not have "right" answers, particularly questions that aim at meaning or application. Instead the questions push us to explore the passage more thoroughly.

When possible, link what you say to the comments of others. Also, be affirming whenever you can. This will encourage some of the more hesitant members of the group to participate.

**5.** Be careful not to dominate the discussion. We are sometimes so eager to express our thoughts that we leave too little opportunity for others to respond. By all means participate! But allow others to also.

**6.** Expect God to teach you through the passage being discussed and through the other members of the group. Pray that you will have an enjoyable and profitable time together, but also that as a result of the study you will find ways that you can take action individually and/or as a group.

**7.** It will be helpful for groups to follow a few basic guidelines. These guidelines, which you may wish to adapt to your situation, should be read at the beginning of the first session.

☐ Anything said in the group is considered confidential and will not be discussed outside the group unless specific permission is given to do so.

☐ We will provide time for each person present to talk if he or she feels comfortable doing so.

☐ We will talk about ourselves and our own situations, avoiding conversation about other people.

☐ We will listen attentively to each other.

☐ We will be very cautious about giving advice.

**8.** If you are the group leader, you will find additional suggestions at the back of the guide.

# 1
# PASSING IT ON

## 1 Thessalonians 1

*T*urning. Serving. Waiting. These are the essentials of Christian conversion. We turn from the various idols of our lives with a decisive break from the past. We serve the living God with the gifts we have been given, experiencing liberation in the present. And we wait for Christ, looking to the future with hopeful expectancy. Without this turning, serving and waiting one can scarcely claim to have been converted.

The news which was spreading far and wide from Thessalonica was that people were turning away from idols to serve the true God and wait for Christ to return. God intends every church to be like a sounding board, bouncing off the vibrations of the gospel, or like a telecommunications satellite which first receives and then transmits messages. In fact, this is God's simplest plan for world evangelization.

## Open

■ What were the ways (at least the ones you are aware of) God used to introduce you to the gospel?

## Study

■ In this first chapter Paul refers to both the church and the gospel. He begins by describing the church of God, which the gospel has brought into being (vv. 1-4), and goes on to describe the gospel of God which the church has received and is spreading (vv. 5-10). Thus the gospel creates the church, which spreads the gospel, which creates more churches, which in their turn spread the gospel further. *Read 1 Thessalonians 1:1-5.*

Paul asserts that he, Silas and Timothy know their brothers and sisters in Thessalonica to have been chosen by God. The doctrine of election, far from making evangelism unnecessary, makes it indispensable. For it is only through the preaching and receiving of the gospel that God's secret purpose comes to be revealed and known. After commending the faith, hope and love of the Thessalonian church, it was natural for Paul to move on in his mind from God's church to God's gospel; he could not think of either without the other. It is by the gospel that the church exists and by the church that the gospel spreads. Each depends on the other. Each serves the other.

**1.** How did Paul express his affection and good will toward the Thessalonian Christians?

**2.** What evidences did Paul find that the Thessalonians had responded to the gospel (v. 3)?

**3.** How is each evidence a reflection of the character of Christ?

**4.** When Paul and his companions preached the gospel to the people of Thessalonica, how was their message supplemented and confirmed?

---

**5.** Which of the elements of verse 5 have you often seen in preaching and witnessing?

---

Which have you observed to be lacking?

*Summary:* The gospel did not come to Thessalonica by itself. It did not drop by parachute from heaven. The planting of the church was the direct result of the preaching of the gospel. The gospel did not come with words only, but it did come by words. Words matter. The gospel has a specific content. In all our evangelism, whether in public preaching or in private witnessing, we need to take trouble with our choice of words. But because words may be misunderstood or disregarded, they need somehow to be enforced by "power" (the objective result of the preaching) and "conviction" (the subjective state of the preacher). The truth of the Word, the conviction with which we speak it, and the power of its impact on others all come from the Holy Spirit. The Spirit without the Word is weaponless; the Word without the Spirit is powerless.

---

**6.** *Read 1 Theassolonians 1:6-10.* When the Thessalonians received the gospel, what was the contrast between their inward and outward condition?

**7.** For what features of their lives had the Thessalonian Christians justly become "famous"?

_____

**8.** The Thessalonians became imitators of Paul, Silas and Timothy as well as imitators of the Lord Jesus Christ. In turn the Thessalonians became models so that others were imitating them. In your spiritual life what Christlike models have you been inspired to imitate?

_____

**9.** The Greek word in verse 8 for "rang out" occurs nowhere else in the New Testament. It is derived from _ēchos,_ an echo or noise. In the Greek translation of the Old Testament it was used of bells, zithers, trumpets and other loud noises. How is this an appropriate metaphor for sharing the good news of Christ?

_____

**10.** After the Thessalonians turned from idols to Christ, they became engaged in serving God and waiting for his Son to return. How are turning, serving and waiting interrelated?

_____

_Summary:_ While we should harness to the service of the gospel every modern communication medium available, there is another very effective way to spread the gospel—simple, spontaneous and without cost. We might call it "holy gossip." It is the excited transmission from mouth to mouth of the impact which the good news is making on people. "Did you know that such and such a person has come to believe in God and has been completely transformed?" Through such communication, we discover that conversion is not only to be regarded in negative terms as a turning away from the old life, but also positively as the beginning of a new life of service.

## Apply ─────────────────────────────
■ Through the Thessalonians, "the Lord's message rang out" in Macedonia and Achaia and beyond. Where are your spheres of influence where the Lord's message can become known through your words and presence?

The Thessalonians turned from idols, served God and waited for Christ. In which of those areas do you feel closest to the Thessalonian church?

In which of those three areas do you feel furthest from the Thessalonian church?

## Pray ─────────────────────────────
■ Thank God for the working of his grace in your life. Pray that the attitude of the Thessalonians will also be your attitude.

# 2
# PLEASING GOD

## 1 Thessalonians 2:1-16

*P*art of the abiding value of 1 Thessalonians 2 and 3 is the insight it gives us into Paul's pastoral heart. In these chapters, more perhaps than anywhere else in his letters, he discloses his mind, expresses his emotions and bares his soul.

Paul's critics in Thessalonica, in order to undermine his authority and his gospel, determined to discredit him by a malicious smear campaign. Paul must have found this personal attack extremely painful. He determined to reply to the charges which were being leveled at him, not out of pique or vanity, but because the truth of the gospel and the future of the church were at stake.

## Open ———————————————————————

■ For whom do you feel a special spiritual affection and concern?

## Study ———————————————————————

■ *Read 1 Thessalonians 2:1-6.* By studying Paul's self-defense, it is possible for us to reconstruct the slanderous words that were said against him: "He's in his job only for what he can get out of it in terms of sex, money, prestige or power. So when opposition arose, and he found himself in personal dangers, he ran! He doesn't care about you Thessalonian disciples of his; he has abandoned you!"

**1.** What positive motives does Paul claim for himself in his preaching?

**2.** What did Paul *not* do in bringing the gospel to the Thessalonians?

**3.** Paul disclaims any impure motives for his preaching. What are some possible impure motives for Christian ministry?

**4.** What is liberating about working not to please people but to please God?

*Summary:* Paul asserted that God had entrusted the gospel to him, as a householder entrusts his property to his steward. Paul insists that his message was true, his motives were pure and his methods were open and above-board. In these three areas his conscience was entirely clear.

God had tested Paul and found him fit. As a result of the successful test, God had entrusted him with the gospel, making him a steward of it. God was the person Paul was trying to please. And God continued to test Paul's heart. The stewards of the gospel are primarily responsible neither to the church nor to its leaders, but to God himself. To be accountable to God is to be delivered from the tyranny of human criticism.

5. *Read 1 Thessalonians 2:6-12.* Paul compares his attitude in ministry among the Thessalonians to both a mother and a father. How does each role call for self-sacrifice or unselfishness?

6. What characteristics of a mother's care for her children are also appropriate for ministry?

7. How have other Christians shared with you not only the gospel but their very lives?

8. What characteristics of a father's care for his children are also appropriate for ministry?

9. How could the "parental" approach to ministry be misused?

*Summary:* Far from using the Thessalonians to minister to himself, Paul gave himself to minister to them. It is a beautiful thing that a man as tough and masculine as the apostle Paul should have applied to himself the metaphor of a mother gently caring for her children. In applying the fatherhood metaphor to himself he seemed to be thinking especially of the educational role of fathers, who should not only set a consistent example but should encourage, comfort and exhort their children. It is impressive that, in his pastoral care of the Thessalonians, Paul could claim to have combined both the father's and the mother's roles.

---

**10.** *Read 1 Thessalonians 2:13-16.* Why was Paul pleased about the Thessalonians' attitude toward the nature of the gospel?

---

**11.** Paul details the Thessalonians' suffering under persecution. How could his words serve as a comfort to the Thessalonian church?

---

**12.** How can we reconcile Paul's harsh words toward nonbelieving Jews with his claim to have the loving attitudes of a mother and a father?

*Summary:* Like a steward Paul was faithful in guarding the gospel; like a mother he was gentle in caring for his converts; like a father he was diligent in educating them; and like a herald he was bold in proclaiming God's word. From these four metaphors we may discern the two major responsibilities of pastoral ministry for today. The first is to the Word of God (as both steward to guard it and herald to proclaim it), and the second to the people of God (as their mother and father, to love, nurture and teach them).

## Apply

■ Think again about people in whose spiritual growth you take a special interest. How do you demonstrate that you care?

Whether you are a layperson or a pastor, how can Paul's example of pastoral care give you practical ideas for caring for "younger" Christians (younger in the faith)?

## Pray

■ Pray for people who are new or immature in Christ. Ask the Lord how you can help give them guidance.

Thank the Lord for people who have taken a sincere interest in your spiritual growth.

# 3
# DOUBLE COMMITMENT

## 1 Thessalonians 2:17—3:13

*E*very authentic Christian ministry begins with the conviction that we have been called to handle God's Word as its guardians and heralds, as Paul emphasizes in 1 Thessalonians 2. We must not be satisfied with "rumors of God" as a substitute for "good news from God." We are trustees of the apostolic faith, which is the Word of God and which works powerfully in those who believe. Our task is to keep it, study it, expound it, apply it and obey it.

Second, there is our commitment to the people of God. In 2:17—3:13 Paul gives a moving illustration of his love for the Thessalonians. He had left them only with the greatest reluctance, and had in fact been torn away from them against his will. He had then tried hard to visit them, but all his attempts had been thwarted. Finally he sent Timothy, leaving himself isolated in Athens in order to learn news of the Thessalonian church. Timothy's good report overwhelmed the apostle with joy, leading him to sit down to write this letter.

## Open
■ Think of a time when you have been separated from a Christian friend

or family member and not heard any word of how that person was doing. How did you feel?

## Study ————————————————————————————

■ *Read 1 Thessalonians 2:17—3:5.* When Paul writes "we were torn away from you," he uses a Greek verb whose only New Testament occurrence is in this verse. *Orphanos* normally means an orphan, a parentless child. The word can also include bereavement in general. The emphasis is on unnatural separation, both forcible and painful. At the same time, Paul felt sure that the separation was only temporary, and he assured them that it was in person but not in thought.

---

**1.** What intense words reveal Paul's feelings for the church in Thessalonica?

---

**2.** How might Paul have kept himself from discouragement when he found his return to Thessalonica blocked?

Why did Paul attribute his blockage from seeing the Thessalonians to Satan, while attributing other such blocks to God (v. 18)? One answer could be that God gave Paul spiritual discernment to distinguish between providential and demonic happenings. It is also possible that this attribution could be made only with the benefit of hindsight because of the way events worked out.

**3.** What did Paul hope to receive (indirectly, through Timothy's report) from the Thessalonians?

**4.** Paul had tried to prepare the Thessalonians for meeting trials. How might his own words have strengthened him as he waited for news from Thessalonica?

**5.** How do you interpret Paul's statement that the Thessalonians would be his hope, joy and crown when Jesus returns?

**6.** In the sense that Paul used the words, who is (or are) your own "hope, joy and crown"?

*Summary:* Paul's repeated efforts to revisit Thessalonica were made more frustrating by the lack of news about the church there. The suspense grew until something had to be done to relieve the tension. So, since Paul could not go himself, the decision was made to send Timothy in his place. Paul's sensitive spirit shrank from the prospect, but he could bear another bout of loneliness better than a further period of suspense over the Thessalonians.

**7.** *Read 1 Thessalonians 3:6-13.* Paul had endured a great deal in establishing the church in Thessalonica. Yet his letter overflows with gratitude. Specifically, what had he received from ministering to the people there?

---

**8.** When Paul wrote that Timothy had just "brought good news," the word he used was literally "evangelized." This is the only time the word is used in the New Testament when it does not specifically refer to preaching of the gospel. Why would news of the Thessalonians' faith and love spur Paul to make such a strong statement?

---

**9.** How did Paul pray for the Thessalonians, and what does his prayer reveal about what he wanted for them?

---

**10.** Consider people who minister to you, whether professionally or as laypeople or just as friends. What might they be receiving from their ministry (beyond professional pay)?

---

**11.** What blessings have you received from ministering to other people?

***Summary:*** Paul lays bare his heart of love for the Thessalonians. Why does he use such extravagant language? It is the language of parents who are separated from their children, who miss them dreadfully and are profoundly anxious when they have no recent news of them. Pastoral love is parental love; that is its quality.

## Apply

■ Deep involvement with others in ministry can lead to pain when there is separation and/or disappointment. Taking this passage as a whole, what do you find in Paul's words to encourage you that the risk of pain is worth it?

How can you return blessings to those who have blessed you through their ministry?

## Pray

■ Thank God for those who have faithfully served you in ministry, and ask God to bless them.

# 4
# LIVING
# THE GOSPEL

## 1 Thessalonians 4:1-12

One of the greatest weaknesses of contemporary Christianity is our comparative neglect of Christian ethics, in both our teaching and our practice. We are known as people who preach the gospel rather than as those who live it. We are not always conspicuous in the community, as we should be, for our respect for the sanctity and the quality of human life, our commitment to social justice, our personal honesty and integrity in business, our simplicity of lifestyle and happy contentment in contrast to the greed of the consumer society, or for the stability of our homes in which unfaithfulness and divorce are practically unknown.

Paul presents a striking contrast to our neglect of ethics, giving detailed instruction in Christian moral behavior even to very young converts. In this part of his letter he urges the Thessalonians to please God, to control themselves and to love one another.

## Open

■ What is one area in which your Christian faith has made a significant difference in your ethics?

## Study

■ Between chapters 3 and 4 of 1 Thessalonians there is an abrupt change of topic. Paul has been looking back to his visit and the following events; now he looks to the present and future of the Thessalonian church and addresses himself to certain practical problems of Christiań conduct. Paul's sudden shift of theme does not mean, however, that there are no links between the first and second parts of his letter. His prayer at the end of chapter 3, that the Lord would cause them to grow in love and holiness, paves the way for his teaching about both in chapter 4.

---

**1.** *Read 1 Thessalonians 4:1-2.* What is the tone of these verses?

---

**2.** What are several reasons a Christian would want to please God?

---

**3.** Why is pleasing God a sound foundation for Christian ethics?

---

**4.** What are some other, not-so-sound foundations on which Christians might attempt to build their ethics?

**Summary:** As a guiding principle of Christian behavior, "pleasing God" is a radical concept. It strikes at the roots of our discipleship and challenges the reality of our profession. How can we claim to know and to love God if we do not seek to please him? At the same time it is a flexible principle. It will rescue us from the rigidities of a Christian Pharisaism which tries to reduce morality to a list of do's and don'ts.

*Read 1 Thessalonians 4:3-8.* Paul was writing from Corinth to Thessalonica, and both cities were famed for their immorality. They were possibly no worse than other Greco-Roman cities of that period, in which it was widely accepted that a man either could not or would not limit himself to his wife as his only sexual partner. Throughout church history commentators have been divided as to the meaning of verse 4; literally translated, it reads that "each of you should learn to acquire his own vessel in holiness and honor." While there are difficulties with rendering the verse either "control his own body" or "take a wife for himself," there are several arguments for accepting that the reference is to acquiring a wife and that Paul is affirming heterosexual marriage.

---

**5.** What is the relationship between Christians' being sanctified or made holy (v. 3) and Christians' sexual behavior?

---

**6.** When are you most aware of the contrast between the sexual standards of Christians and those of the world?

---

**7.** In sexual matters, what are several ways a Christian could "wrong" or "take advantage of" another believer (v. 6)?

**8.** What motivates a Christian to live by God's principles for sexuality?

*Summary:* Paul presents two fundamental, practical principles to guide his readers in their sexual behavior: (1) sex has a God-given context: heterosexual marriage; (2) sex has a God-given style: holiness and honor. If the heathen behave as they do because they do not know God, Christians must behave in a completely different way because we do know God, because he is a holy God, because he is our God and because we want to please him. *Read 2 Thessalonians 4:9-12.*

From other references in 1 and 2 Thessalonians, it is apparent that there was a group in the Thessalonian church who had abandoned their jobs, perhaps because they thought the Lord's return was imminent. They needed to be exhorted to go back to their work.

---

**9.** How do Christians learn what it means to love each other?

---

**10.** What "ambition" are Christians to have, according to verses 11-12?

---

**11.** What spiritual dangers do we avoid when we live quietly and mind our own business?

**12.** How is working for one's own living a mark of Christian love?

**13.** As we try to win the respect of nonbelievers, how can we avoid compromising our principles?

*Summary:* Christian morality is not primarily rules and regulations, but relationships. On the one hand, the more we know and love God, the more we shall want to please him. We are to develop a spiritual sensitivity toward God, through his Word and Spirit, until in every dilemma it becomes safe and practical to ask ourselves, "Would it please him?" On the other hand, love for others leads us to serve them. Whatever we wish others would do to us, we shall want to do to them. It is a wonderfully liberating experience when the desire to please God overtakes the desire to please ourselves, and when love for others displaces self-love.

## Apply ————————————————————————

■ Consider ways in which you need to grow in your love for your fellow Christians so that you love them "more and more." Think of expanding two different circles:

(1) general areas of service and ministry

(2) specific people you accept and are concerned for

How might your daily life command the respect of outsiders?

What changes will you make so that you increasingly win the respect of nonbelievers?

## Pray

■ Ask God to grow your behavior to match your beliefs so that others might see your love for God and for the people around you.

# 5
# HOPE IN THE FACE OF DEATH

## *1 Thessalonians 4:13-18*

*H*owever firm our Christian faith may be, the loss of a close relative or friend causes a profound emotional shock. To lose a loved one is to lose a part of oneself. It calls for radical and painful adjustments, which may take many months.

Bereavement also occasions anguished questions about those who have died. What has happened to them? Are they all right? Will we see them again? Such questions arise partly from a natural curiosity, partly from Christian concern for the dead, and partly because their death reminds us of our own mortality and undermines our security. In this portion of 1 Thessalonians Paul encourages the Thessalonians, who were anxious about their Christian friends who had died.

## Open
What feelings or thoughts come over you when you think about Christians you love who have died?

## Study

■ *Read 1 Thessalonians 4:13-18.* Paul had taught the Thessalonians that the Lord Jesus was going to reappear in order to take his people home to himself. There is no evidence that Paul led the Thessalonians to believe that Christ would return in their lifetime. But they seem to have been expecting him so soon that some had given up their jobs, while others were totally unprepared to see relatives or friends die before Christ's advent. Either directly or through Timothy, the Thessalonians asked Paul: Would the Christian dead miss the blessing of Christ's coming? Were they even lost?

**1.** What reasons for Christians to have hope are mentioned here?

**2.** Paul did not want the Thessalonians to be ignorant about the fate of those who had died. What are the spiritual dangers of ignorance about life after death?

**3.** The death of someone we love naturally causes grief. If Paul is not telling Christians not to grieve at all, then what is he telling us about grieving for Christians who have died?

**4.** Today, two thousand years after Christ's ascension, we take it for granted that many Christians will have lived and died between Christ's first and second comings. Why would the Thessalonians have been upset that some in the church had died and Christ had not yet returned?

---

**5.** There are many details about Jesus' second coming which the Bible does not tell us. What details are revealed here?

---

**6.** How does true Christian hope extend beyond this life?

---

**7.** Paul refers to people who have died as having "fallen asleep." There are other places in the Bible where death is referred to as "sleep." The Greek word which is the basis for "cemetery" is literally a sleeping place. What are several reasons that the state of death could be referred to as "sleep"?

---

**8.** How would you contrast Christian hope with some popular views of life after death?

---

**9.** How can our Christian hope affect our natural fear of death?

---

**10.** Paul says there is also a great hope for those who are still living when Christ returns. What is that hope?

**11.** Various Christian groups have had various views of the end times and what will happen at Christ's return. Churches have even split over end-time issues. In contrast to arguing, how can the promised return of Christ be a source of unity for Christians (v. 18)?

*Summary:* If God did not abandon Jesus to death, he will not abandon the Christian dead either. On the contrary, he will raise them as he raised him, and he will bring them with him, so that when he comes, they will come too. What Paul is affirming is that neither the Christian dead nor the Christian living will be left behind or excluded or disadvantaged in any way. Having been caught up to meet the Lord, we shall be with the Lord forever. The momentary encounter will lead to an everlasting fellowship.

## Apply

■ Who do you know who needs the hope spelled out in this passage? How can you be God's instrument of hope for that person?

Perhaps you are undergoing grief over a Christian's death, whether recent or some time ago. How does this passage encourage you and affect your ideas and feelings?

## Pray

■ Praise the Lord for the certainty of his return and for his gift of hope.

# 6
# WAITING
# FOR CHRIST

## 1 Thessalonians 5:1-11

*T*here are two reasons why people are taken by surprise when a burglar breaks in. The first is that the burglar comes unexpectedly during the night, and the second is that the householder is asleep. We can do nothing about the first reason, but we can about the second.

The Thessalonians thought they could most easily get ready for Christ's coming in judgment if they could know when he would arrive. It was naive, to be sure, but perfectly understandable. Paul responds that the solution to their problem does not lie in knowing the date. Christ's coming is definitely going to be unexpected. The solution is not in knowing when he will come, but in staying awake and alert.

## Open

■ What place does the expectation of Christ's return have in your Christian life and experience? (Is it something you think of frequently or rarely? Do you think about how it will happen? what it will be like?)

## Study

■ Paul is clear that the solution to the church's problems is to be found in the gospel. In order to embolden the faint heart of the Thessalonians, he aims to stimulate their Christian hope by developing the theology on which it rests. This hope is the confident expectation of Christ's second coming, and this theology is the truth that the Christ who is coming is the same Christ who died and rose again, in whom they had put their trust.

---

**1.** *Read 1 Thessalonians 5:1-3.* What concerns is Paul addressing in these verses?

---

**2.** Ever since Christ ascended, people have tried to predict when he will return. What is so appealing about pinning down the date of Christ's second coming?

---

**3.** How will the Lord's coming be like the coming of a nighttime burglar?

---

**4.** How will the Lord's coming be like the onset of labor for a pregnant woman?

---

**5.** Some people try to predict the exact time of Christ's return, while others scoff at the idea that it could be soon. How does Paul's statement that Christ will come unexpectedly counter both errors?

*Summary:* Putting Paul's two metaphors together, we may say that Christ's coming will be (1) sudden and unexpected (like a burglar in the night) and (2) sudden and unavoidable (like labor at the end of pregnancy). In the first case there will be no warning, and in the second no escape. But just as Paul had already told the Thessalonians when he was with them, no one knows or will know the exact time.

*Read 1 Thessalonians 5:4-11.* The Bible divides history into two ages or eons. From the Old Testament perspective they were called "the present age" (which was evil) and "the age to come" (which would be the time of the Messiah). The Bible also teaches that Jesus Christ is that long-awaited Messiah, and that therefore the new age began when he came. At the same time, the old age has not yet come to an end. So for the time being, the two ages overlap. Unbelievers belong to the old age and are still in the darkness. But those who belong to Jesus Christ have been transferred into the new age, into the light. Only when Christ comes in glory will the present overlap the end. The old age will finally vanish, and the new age will be consummated.

---

**6.** Describe the attitudes and behavior of those who are still in spiritual darkness.

---

**7.** How do the attitudes and behavior of those who belong to the light contrast with those who belong to the darkness?

**8.** What are some spiritual traps which Christians should stay alert for?

**9.** Paul refers to faith and love as a breastplate and the hope of salvation as a helmet. Why does a Christian need these pieces of armor?

**10.** How does Paul express confidence that the Thessalonians will be ready when Christ returns?

**11.** How does Paul once again reassure the Thessalonians about those who had died?

**12.** Why do we need encouragement from each other as we wait for Christ to return?

*Summary:* Whether we are ready for Christ's coming or not depends on which age we belong to, on whether we are still in the darkness or already belong to the light. It is only if we are in the light that we will not be taken by surprise. If we belong to the day (the new day which dawned with Christ), our behavior must be daytime behavior. Let's not sleep or even yawn our way through life, or live in our pajamas. Let's stay awake and alert. For then we shall be ready when Christ comes, and we will not be taken by surprise.

The ultimate reason we should be bold rather than faint-hearted in anticipation of the second coming lies not in who we are (children of the day and of the light) but on who God is, as revealed in the cross (the giver of salvation and life). The fact that Christ is coming can cause anxiety rather than reassurance. Reassurance comes from knowing that the Christ who is coming to us is the very same Christ who died for us and rose again.

## Apply

■ In what ways might you be still yawning your way through life and not living in the full light of Christ?

How can you encourage someone today with the hope of Christ's return?

## Pray

■ Thank God for delivering you from his wrath and giving you salvation in Christ.

# 7
# CHRISTIAN COMMUNITY

## *1 Thessalonians 5:12-18*

*T*he apostle Paul cherished high ideals for the Christian church. In 1 Thessalonians he describes it as a community loved and chosen by God, drawing its life from him and manifesting this divine life in the basic Christian graces of faith, love and hope. Such a community could justly be called a "gospel church," both because it has been brought into being by the gospel and because it is continuously shaped by the gospel.

One New Testament picture of a gospel church portrays it as the family of God, whose members recognize and treat one another as sisters and brothers. This seems to be the key concept in the second half of 1 Thessalonians 5, since five times Paul uses the word *brothers* (which includes "sisters," in the one "brotherhood"). Here Paul takes up one by one three essential aspects of the life of the local church: leadership, fellowship and public worship.

## Open ———————————————————————

■ How are you helped and encouraged by your Christian "family"?

## Study

■ *Read 1 Thessalonians 5:12-13.* The church of Jesus Christ has oscillated unsteadily between the equally unbiblical extremes regarding the role of pastors. In one view the clergy monopolize all pastoral leadership and are put on a pedestal, receiving an exaggerated deference from the so-called laity. At the opposite extreme is an overreaction which takes the legitimate model of the church as the body of Christ and presses it to the extreme position that clergy in any shape or form are redundant. According to the New Testament, the Chief Shepherd delegates to undershepherds or "pastors" the privileged oversight of the flock which he has purchased with his own blood.

---

**1.** According to this passage, what are the responsibilities of church leaders toward those they lead?

---

**2.** What are the responsibilities of those they lead?

---

**3.** How do Paul's instructions preclude either pastors or laypeople "lording it over" each other?

---

**4.** Why do pastors and laypeople sometimes find it difficult to live in peace with each other?

*Summary:* The chief characteristic of Christian leaders is humility, not authority, and gentleness, not power. Nevertheless, authentic servant-leadership still carries an element of authority. The local congregation should neither despise pastors as if they were dispensable, nor flatter and fawn on them as if they were popes or princes, but should rather respect them with a combination of appreciation and affection.

*Read 1 Thessalonians 5:14-15.* Earlier in his letter, in 4:3-18, Paul had dealt with daily work, bereavement and sexual self-control. Perhaps those are the three topics he had in mind when he wrote "warn those who are idle, encourage the timid [or faint-hearted], help the weak." The existence of pastors does not relieve church members of their responsibilities to care for one another, including these "problem children" of the church family.

---

**5.** What attitudes does Paul encourage between believers?

---

**6.** Why do the idle, the timid and the weak especially need patience from others in the church?

---

**7.** What sort of people (or problems of people) make you impatient?

---

**8.** Paul could have written, "Don't pay back wrong for wrong." Instead he wrote, "Make sure that nobody pays back wrong for wrong." (Remember that he was addressing church members at large and not pastors.) What is implied in his command?

---

**9.** When wrongs are "paid back" with kindness rather than with further wrongs, what problems are warded off?

*Summary:* Paul lays on the whole congregation the responsibility to care for each other as sisters and brothers, to give appropriate support, encouragement or admonition to the church's problem children, and to ensure that all its members follow the teaching of Jesus, cultivating patience, renouncing retaliation and pursuing kindness.

*Read 1 Thessalonians 5:16-28.* At first reading one might not think that this section relates to the nature and conduct of public worship. But there are clear indications that this is primarily what Paul had in mind. All the verbs are plural, so that they seem to describe our collective and public, rather than individual and private, Christian duties.

Most churches could afford to give more time and trouble to the preparation of their worship. It is a mistake to imagine either that freedom and form exclude one another, or that the Holy Spirit is the friend of freedom in such a way as to be the enemy of form.

**10.** What attitudes are affirmed in this passage?

**11.** How do joy in the Lord, prayer and thankfulness fit with public worship?

**12.** What standards do you use to test whether a message or a messenger is from the Holy Spirit?

**13.** How does Paul express confidence in God's faithfulness?


**14.** After making many authoritative statements, Paul asks the Thessalonians to pray for him. What does Paul's request tell you about his spirit?


*Summary:* It is God's will, as expressed and seen in Jesus Christ, whenever his people meet together for worship, and whatever their feelings and circumstances may be, that there should be rejoicing in him, praying to him and giving him thanks for his mercies. When a message purports to come from God, we should neither reject nor accept it outright but listen to it, sift it and weigh carefully what is said. In all this, the living out of brotherly and sisterly love in the local church is possible only by the gracious work of God.

## Apply ————————————————————————————
■ Who in your church fellowship needs your support and patience?


Using this Scripture passage for inspiration, how could you pray for your pastor and other leaders in your church?



## Pray ————————————————————————————
■ Thank God for his faithfulness to you. Recommit yourself to trust him to keep you spiritually safe and whole. Pray for your pastor.

# 8
# DYNAMIC FAITH

## 2 Thessalonians 1

We tend to speak of faith in static terms as something we either have or do not have. "I wish I had your faith," we say, like "I wish I had your complexion," as if it were a genetic endowment. Or we complain "I've lost my faith" like "I've lost my spectacles," as if it were a commodity. But faith is a relationship of trust in God, and like all relationships is a living, dynamic, growing thing. It is similar with love. We assume rather helplessly that we either love somebody or we do not, and that we can do nothing about it. But love also, like faith, is a living relationship, whose growth we can take steps to nurture.

In 2 Thessalonians we see that Paul's earlier prayer that their love might "increase and overflow" (1 Thessalonians 3:12) and his vision that they would love each other "more and more" (1 Thessalonians 4:10) were being fulfilled. Their faith was also growing.

## Open ──────────────────────────────
■ When have you struggled with feeling your faith is "inadequate"?

## Study ──────────────────────────────
**1.** *Read 2 Thessalonians 1:1-4.* What do you learn about Paul's relationship

with the Thessalonians from these verses?

**2.** Paul thanked God for the Thessalonians' increasing faith and love. For whose faith and love are you thankful?

**3.** What gave Paul the right to "boast" about the Thessalonians?

**4.** Persecutions and trials sometimes lead to increased perseverance and faith, but not always. What makes the difference?

*Summary:* What should our attitude be toward Christians who are doing well in some aspect of their discipleship? There is a way to affirm people without spoiling them. Paul not only thanks God for the Thessalonians; he also tells them that he is doing so. This way affirms without flattering and encourages without puffing up.

**5.** *Read 2 Thessalonians 1:5-10.* What is included in the "evidence that God's judgment is just"?

It takes spiritual discernment to see in a situation of injustice evidence of the just judgment of God. Our habit is to see only the surface appearance, and so make only superficial comments. We see the malice, cruelty, power and arrogance of the persecutors. We see the sufferings of the people of God. In other words, what we see is injustice—the wicked flourishing and the righteous suffering. "Why doesn't God do something?" we complain indignantly.

---

**6.** How and when will God demonstrate his justice?

---

**7.** Using all five of your senses, describe the scene when Jesus is revealed from heaven.

---

**8.** The scenario which Paul describes is a furious and terrible one. What makes it a hopeful scenario for Christians?

**Summary:** Since God was allowing the Thessalonians to suffer, they could know that he was preparing them for glory. Their suffering was itself evidence of the justice of God, because it was the first part of the equation which guaranteed that the second part (glory) would follow. The coming of Christ will be no petty, local sideshow; it will be an event of awe-inspiring, cosmic splendor.

**9.** *Read 2 Thessalonians 1:11-12.* What is "this" which Paul keeps in mind and which inspires him to prayer?

---

**10.** We can never be worthy of Jesus Christ. How do you reconcile that fact with Paul's prayer that God would "count you worthy of his calling"?

---

**11.** Consider the various things Paul prays for the Thessalonians. How would each help them endure persecution and wait for Christ's coming?

**Prayer**                                   **How It Builds Endurance**

---

**12.** Notice the ultimate purpose Paul cites for his prayer for the Thessalonians (v. 12). What does this mean?

---

How does it help in defining your purpose in life?

*Summary:* When by God's power God's people live a life worthy of his call, and when their resolve issues in goodness and their faith in works, then Jesus himself is seen and honored in them, and through union with him they are seen in their true humanness as the image of God.

## Apply —————————————————————

■ How are you affected by the prospect of Christ's coming in judgment?

What would help you—or does help you—to feel ready?

## Pray —————————————————————

■ Thank God for the faith and love of other believers whose lives have touched yours. Praise God that you will be delivered when Christ comes in judgment. If the thought of his coming fills you with apprehension, ask God for reassurance about your salvation.

# 9
# STANDING FIRM

## 2 Thessalonians 2

*T*he intellectual assault on Christianity is often fiercer than the physical. To be sure, both kinds of challenge can be beneficial, like the refining of precious metals in the fire. But both can also be painful and cause havoc. False teachers as well as persecutors were disturbing the peace of the Thessalonian church, and Paul took them on in chapter 2.

## Open

■ How do you respond when you see Christians upset and unsettled by false teachings?

## Study

**1.** *Read 2 Thessalonians 2:1-3.* When Paul wrote his first letter to the Thessalonians, they were troubled that the Lord's coming had not happened quickly enough; now their concern was that he had already come. What words and phrases suggest the frame of mind of the Thessalonians?

**2.** How did Paul counteract the false teaching that the day of the Lord had already come?

---

**3.** What must take place before the day of the Lord?

---

**4.** Although Paul does not call the person named in verse 3 the "antichrist," this is evidently who he is. Regarding the identity of the "man of lawlessness," here we should have humility. Church history is littered with mistaken attempts to find in Paul's text a reference to some contemporary person and event. What do we learn about this person from verse 3?

In countering the false teaching that the day of the Lord had already arrived, Paul's essential point was that the rebellion will precede Christ's return. He does not deny that the return of the Lord will be sudden and, to those unprepared for it, unexpected. But, as he argued in his first letter, it will not take believers by surprise.

Paul had already told the Thessalonians all this and more about the coming man of lawlessness. The safeguard against deception and the remedy against false teaching were to hold on to the original teaching of the apostle. The Thessalonians must neither imagine that Paul had changed his mind nor swallow ideas that were incompatible with what he had taught them, even if it was claimed that these ideas came from Paul. Loyalty to apostolic teaching, now permanently enshrined in the New Testament, is still the test of truth and the shield against error.

**5.** *Read 2 Thessalonians 2:4-12.* What is especially repulsive about the behavior of the coming man of lawlessness?

**6.** Paul does not specifically identify what or who is holding back the man of lawlessness. What can be said for sure about this unnamed restraining power (whether pressure or person)?

What is holding back the man of lawlessness? Three main explanations have been proposed. The first suggestion is that the restraining power is the Holy Spirit and the work of the church. The second is Paul and the preaching of the gospel. The third and most widely held view is that the restraining influence is Rome and the power of the state.

**7.** What will happen when the restraining influence is removed?

**8.** By what means will the lawless one deceive people?

**9.** Why will certain people be ripe to be deceived (vv. 9-12)?

**10.** How will the Lord Jesus deal with the lawless one?

**Summary:** According to Paul, the final rebellion will take place publicly and visibly on the stage of history. It will be seen in a worldwide breakdown of the rule of law, of the administration of justice and of the practice of true religion. The coming of the antichrist will be a deliberate and unscrupulous parody of the second coming of Christ. But after a mercifully short period of political, social and moral chaos, Jesus will come and overthrow the antichrist.

In the next section Paul turns from warning of Satan's activity to thanksgiving for God's work, from history and its chaos to eternity and its security. *Read 2 Thessalonians 2:13-17.*

**11.** *Read 2 Thessalonians 2:13-17.* What were the sources of Paul's gratitude for the Thessalonians?

**12.** Of what was Paul confident?

**13.** What would give stability to the Thessalonian church?

**Summary:** In spite of present and future tribulation, Paul feels no panic and adopts no panic measures. On the contrary, he expresses his assured thankfulness to God. His confidence in the stability of the Thessalonians is due entirely to his confidence in the stability of God's loving purpose for them. It is only because God is steadfast that they—and we—can be steadfast too.

## Apply

■ In what ways do you already see political, social and moral chaos at work around you?

What are some areas where you need to stand firm in the midst of chaos?

## Pray

■ Give praise to Jesus that he will have the ultimate victory over sinful rebellion.

# 10
# THE WORD
# OF PEACE

*2 Thessalonians 3*

*D*uring the interim period between the two comings of Christ, while he is absent from the world, God has not left his people without a guiding light or a compass. On the contrary, he has given us both in Scripture. As Paul concludes his second letter to the Thessalonians, he sees the present period before the return of Christ as the era of the Word. First, the church must spread the Word throughout the world. Second, the church must itself obey the Word, conforming its own life to the teaching of the apostles.

## Open
■ What are some signs that the world is in need of Christ?

## Study
■ *Read 2 Thessalonians 3:1-5.* By the words "Finally, brothers" Paul indicates that he is about to take up his last topic; but before he does, he

issues an appeal to his readers to keep on praying for him and his mission team. It is a mark of Paul's humility that he asked for their prayers at the end of his first letter and now repeats his request.

**1.** What are the concerns occupying Paul, which he asks the Thessalonians to pray about (vv. 1-2)?

**2.** How does the church today need the same things which Paul asked the Thessalonians to pray for?

**3.** In the midst of pressing needs, what is Paul confident about (vv. 3-5)?

**4.** Why does continuing obedience to the gospel require both God's love and Christ's perseverance?

*Summary:* Paul urges his readers to pray that the gospel may run in every direction and be welcomed. But is it one thing for the gospel to win friends who embrace it; it is another for the evangelists to be rescued from its enemies who oppose it, and Paul also asks for prayer for deliverance. Meanwhile behind Paul's preaching and the Thessalonians' prayers stands the faithful Lord himself. God will not allow either his Word or his church to fail.

A majority of commentators consider that the reason some in the Thessalonian church were idle was their belief in the imminence of Christ's return. Paul had told them in his first letter to return to work, but evidently his directions had not been heeded.

**5.** *Read 2 Thessalonians 3:6-15.* How would you describe the tone of these verses?

**6.** Paul does not address the idle people directly, except perhaps in verse 12. Instead, how does he approach the problem of their idleness?

**7.** How can the apparent harshness of Paul's commands be justified?

**8.** How does Paul soften the harshness of his instructions?

**9.** In contrast to the idle people in Thessalonica, what example had Paul and his companions set while they stayed there?

Paul lays down five practical guidelines on when, why and how church discipline should be exercised. (1) The need for discipline arises not from some trivial offense but from a public, deliberate and persistent disobedience. (2) The nature of the discipline is a withdrawal of intimate association, though the offender is still regarded as a Christian brother or sister. (3) The entire church body shares responsibility for administering discipline. (4) The spirit in which discipline is administered must be friendly, not hostile. (5) The purpose of discipline is not to humiliate but to lead the offender to repentance and reinstatement.

**10.** How do you respond to the idea of church discipline as it is defined above?

*Read 2 Thessalonians 3:16-18.* The serious division between the workers and the loafers is threatening to split the Thessalonian church. There is a real possibility that disciplinary action may have to be taken. But Paul ardently hopes that the offending church members will repent without the need for discipline. So he pronounces a threefold blessing from Christ upon his church, which takes the form of being half prayer, half wish.

**11.** In what senses is Jesus the "Lord of peace"?

**12.** What is especially gracious about Paul's wish that the Lord will be with "all of you"?

**13.** Drawing on the whole of what you have studied, why was grace especially needed in the church at Thessalonica?

*Summary:* One cannot read the last three verses of this letter without earnestly desiring for the contemporary church what Paul desired for the

Thessalonian church, namely the peace, the presence and the grace of the Lord. Is it possible? Only if we share Paul's perspective on the primacy of the Word in the life of the church. Fully committed to the Lord and his Word, we can humbly expect to enjoy in our day his peace, his presence and his grace.

## Apply

■ Think of someone you know who tends toward idleness, whether because the Lord may return soon or for some other reason. How can you help that person take more initiative?

Are there any ways in which you tend toward idleness? How do Paul's words inspire you to change?

## Pray

■ Pray for the Lord's peace, presence and grace on your own church or fellowship.

# Guidelines for Leaders

*My grace is sufficient for you. (2 Corinthians 12:9)*

If leading a small group is something new for you, don't worry. These sessions are designed to be led easily. Because the Bible study questions flow from observation to interpretation to application, you may feel as if the studies lead themselves.

You don't need to be an expert on the Bible or a trained teacher to lead a small group discussion. As a leader, you can guide group members to discover for themselves what the Bible has to say and to listen for God's guidance. This method of learning will allow group members to remember much more of what is said than a lecture would.

This study guide is flexible. You can use it with a variety of groups—students, professionals, neighborhood or church groups. Each study takes forty-five to sixty minutes in a group setting.

There are some important facts to know about group dynamics and encouraging discussion. The suggestions listed below should equip you to effectively and enjoyably fulfill your role as leader.

### Preparing for the Study

**1.** Ask God to help you understand and apply the passage in your own life. Unless this happens, you will not be prepared to lead others. Pray too for the various members of the group. Ask God to open your hearts to the message of his Word and motivate you to action.

**2.** Read the introduction to the entire guide to get an overview of the topics that will be explored.

**3.** As you begin each study, read and reread the assigned Bible passage to familiarize yourself with it.

**4.** This study guide is based on the New International Version of the Bible. It will help you and the group if you use this translation as the basis for your study and discussion.

**5.** Carefully work through each question in the study. Spend time in meditation and reflection as you consider how to respond.

**6.** Write your thoughts and responses in the space provided in the study guide. This will help you to express your understanding of the passage clearly.

**7.** You may want to get a copy of the Bible Speaks Today commentary by John Stott that supplements the Bible book you are studying. The commentary is divided into short units on each section of Scripture so you can easily read the appropriate material each week. This will help you answer tough questions about the passage and its context.

It may help to have a Bible dictionary handy. Use it to look up any unfamiliar words, names or places. (For additional help on how to study a passage, see *How to Lead a LifeGuide Bible Study* from InterVarsity Press, USA.)

**8.** Take the "Apply" portion of each study seriously. Consider how you need to apply the Scripture to your life. Remember that the group members will follow your lead in responding to the studies. They will not go any deeper than you do.

### Leading the Study

**1.** Begin the study on time. Open with prayer, asking God to help the group to understand and apply the passage.

**2.** Be sure that everyone in your group has a study guide. Encourage the group to prepare beforehand for each discussion by reading the introduction to the guide and by working through the questions in each study.

**3.** At the beginning of your first time together, explain that these studies are meant to be discussions, not lectures. Encourage the members of the group to participate. However, do not put pressure on those who may be hesitant to speak during the first few sessions.

**4.** Have a group member read aloud the introduction at the beginning of the discussion.

**5.** Every session begins with an "open" question, which is meant to be asked before the passage is read. These questions are designed to introduce the theme of the study and encourage group members to begin to open up. Encourage as many members as possible to participate, and be ready to get the discussion going with your own response.

These opening questions can reveal where our thoughts or feelings need to be transformed by Scripture. That is why it is especially important not to read the passage before the question is asked. The passage will tend to color the honest reactions people would otherwise give because they are, of course, supposed to think the way the Bible does.

**6.** Have a group member read aloud the passage to be studied.

**7.** As you ask the study questions, keep in mind that they are designed to be used just as they are written. You may simply read them aloud. Or you may prefer to express them in your own words.

There may be times when it is appropriate to deviate from the study guide. For example, a question may have already been answered. If so, move on to the next question. Or someone may raise an important question not covered in the guide. Take time to discuss it, but try to keep the group from going off on tangents.

**8.** Avoid answering your own questions. If necessary repeat or rephrase them until they are clearly understood. Or point the group to the commentary woven into the guide to clarify the context or meaning without answering the question. An eager group quickly becomes passive and silent if members think the leader will do most of the talking.

**9.** Don't be afraid of silence in response to the discussion questions. People may need time to think about the question before formulating their answers.

**10.** Don't be content with just one answer. Ask, "What do the rest of you think?" or "Anything else?" until several people have given answers to the question.

**11.** Acknowledge all contributions. Try to be affirming whenever possible. Never reject an answer. If it is clearly off-base, ask, "Which verse led you to that conclusion?" or again, "What do the rest of you think?"

**12.** Don't expect every answer to be addressed to you, even though this will probably happen at first. As group members become more at ease, they will begin to truly interact with each other. This is one sign of healthy discussion.

**13.** Don't be afraid of controversy. It can be very stimulating. If you don't resolve an issue completely, don't be frustrated. Explain that the group will move on and God may enlighten all of you in later sessions.

**14.** Periodically summarize what the group has said about the passage. This helps to draw together the various ideas mentioned and gives continuity to the study. But don't preach.

**15.** Conclude your time together with conversational prayer, adapting the prayer suggestion at the end of the study to your group. Ask for God's help in following through on the commitments you've made.

**16.** End on time.

Many more suggestions and helps can be found in *How to Lead a LifeGuide Bible Study* and *The Big Book on Small Groups* (both from InterVarsity Press, USA) or *Housegroups* (Crossway Book, UK). Reading through one of these books would be worth your time.

# For Further Reading
## from InterVarsity Press

### *The Bible Speaks Today by John Stott*
The books in this practical and readable series are companions to the John Stott Bible Studies. They provide further background and insight into the passages.

*The Message of Acts*
*The Message of Ephesians*
*The Message of Galatians*
*The Message of Romans* (UK title), *Romans* (US title)
*The Message of the Sermon on the Mount* (Matthew 5—7)
*The Message of 1 & 2 Thessalonians*
*The Message of 1 Timothy & Titus* (UK title), *Guard the Truth* (US title)
*The Message of 2 Timothy*